RESERVOIR

RESERVOIR

ZAN AGZIGIAN

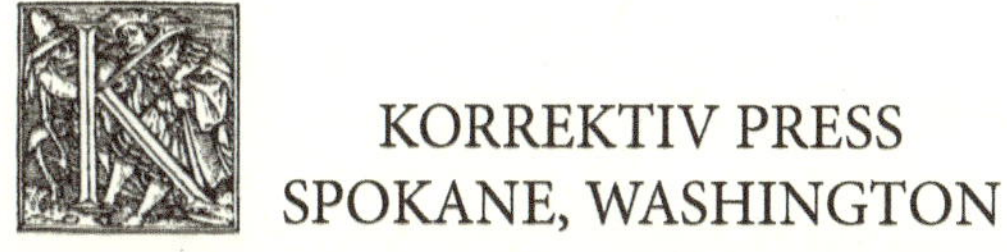

KORREKTIV PRESS
SPOKANE, WASHINGTON

THANKS to Tom I. Davis for his insightful raw edit of this manuscript in its early conception. Rest in peace, Tom; to Dennis Held for his intuitive, compassionate, and deeply intelligent edit of the final manuscript; and to Jonathan Potter of Korrektiv Press for his support.

Poems in this manuscript have also appeared in:

WA State Eco-Map Project, "Pilgrimage to Turnbull," ecopoetrywashington.weebly.com/the-map.html; *Bright Bones: Anthology of Montana Writers,* "Pattee Canyon" and "Pattee Canyon Revisited," brightbonesmontana.wordpress.com/blog; *Pictures of Poets Sound Project* (recorded poems), "Bowie Dawn," picturesofpoets.com/Poets/zan-deery/; *Weird Sisters Lilac City Fairytales, Vol 3, 2017,* "Plains Fair: Late Summer, Montana"; *Down River, Deep Root: A Spokane Anthology,* "On the Banks of Latah Creek, Vinegar Flats: A Love Poem for ItZy BitZ" and "4th of July: Hot Springs."

Cover image: *Sun Lakes* by Bill Kostelec.

"*Sun Lakes* was photographed on an Eastman 2D 5x7 camera from the 1940s using a 1935 Kodak anastigmat lens that came from my dad's 616 Vigilant roll film camera. Thus the lens does not have an image circle big enough for the 5x7 film. The image is a crop from that negative, enlarged on a Beseler 5x7 enlarger. Lens technology was already highly advanced by the 1920s, lacking only the coatings that would by the end of WWII increase light transmission and contrast. The Kodak anastigmat rendered the paradoxical sense of time and timelessness of these ancient cliffs scoured by ice age floods leaving the patina of enduring like the lines of an old man's face. The Wisdom of Rock and the Life of Water." B.K.

Thoth images throughout interior from Adobe Stock

Interior and cover design by Jodi Miller-Hunter

Library of Congress Control Number: 2026940083

ISBN 978-1-962934-04-6

Published by Korrektiv Press, korrektivpress.carrd.co

FOR MY SIBLINGS
Bill, David, and Susan
who added texture to my life
along the Way—
and for my girl,
ItZy BitZy
Unconditional

Kōri toke
yoku mizu kiyoshi
mune kiyoshi

Winter ice
melts into clean water—
clear is my heart

Hyakka

CONTENTS

I (a)

I

II

III

IV

V

VI

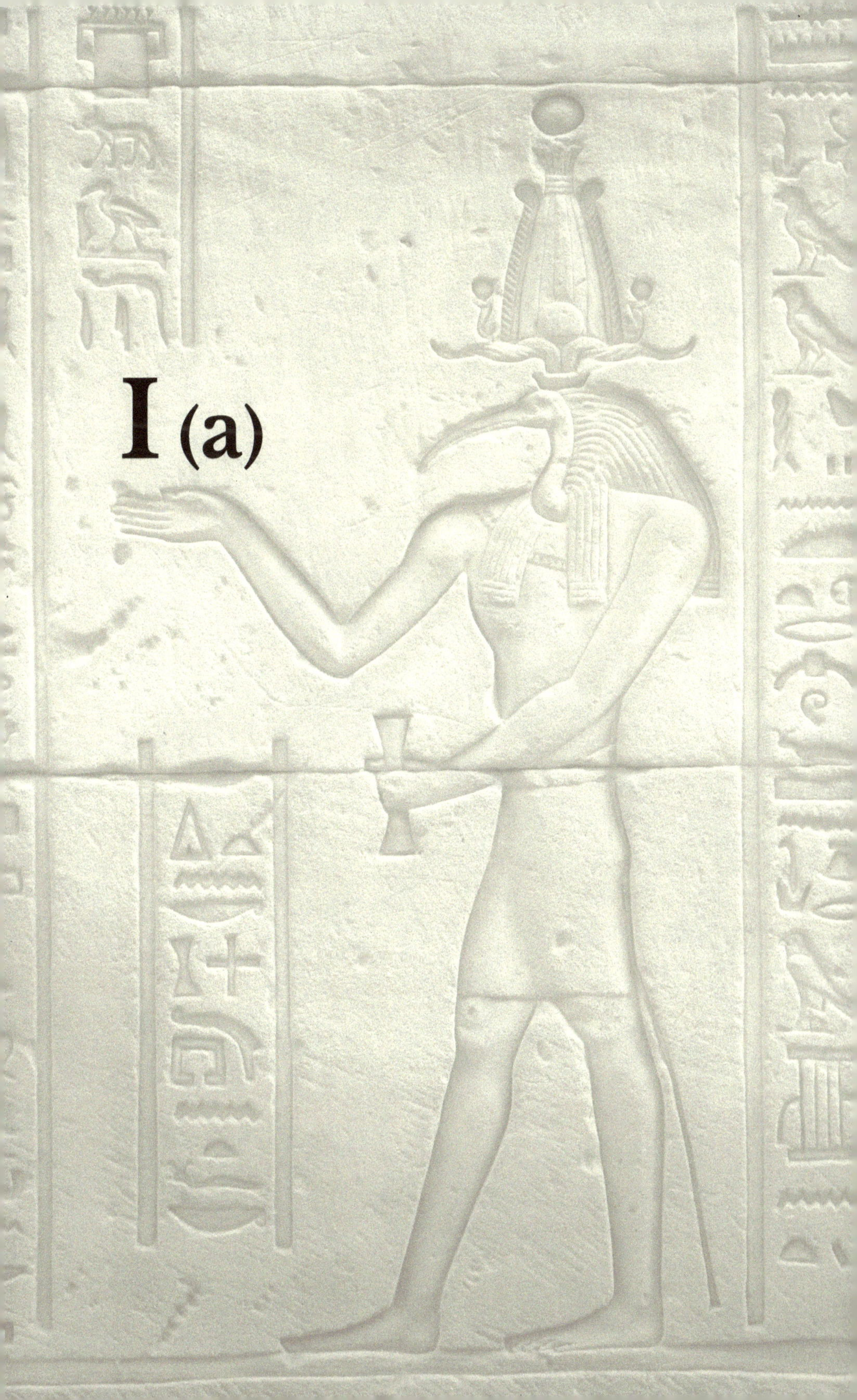
I (a)

THE JOKE

for Jodi, pregnant with Jeram, minding Jacob, caretaking an orchard on the Central CA Coast

It's like parenting
a mountain goat
grabbing for the kid on CA coastal cliff
nothing but slippery rock and concrete
stout dense brush
to cushion potential tumbles
before anticipation disappears
forever into breaking water: tide
through breath of phone
i want to fall into yourbelly
(a plump redclay oven)
ripe motherlode of temperature
where your boy is almost done
taking up room at the inn
you want it to be a "Jesus
let's get outta here" birth
an abscond: no drugs no stress
just emphatic relief
a huge hallelujah push
with sigh of stars
spilling out across sheets
a milky way of blood
a clustered vineyard of drunk
husbandry of James surfing your placenta
sibling Jacob understanding "Welcome,
you will love it here in tow,
new brother, here is
our mother and father—
Just cry for them. They listen
when you're hungry.
When you fall,
they will teach

you to chew arnica.
Whenyoubawl
discomfort,
we will carry the pain."

4TH OF JULY: HOT SPRINGS

for Phoebe Bosche

I promise Phoebe the campout of her life, drive us through a string of switchbacks up and up into the Olympics, the trees more dense, the sky becomes a crack. Rain begins as we park our car in a line of cars. Must be a popular place: Cul de Sol--so wet all you want to do is quack. We trek up a barren trail wondering where all the bodies are: underneath the roots, whisper *I can feel them here, the sunken people.* Climbing higher in a spiral, we spin toward light, up and up to where the trail becomes a strip, and the overhang is a cliff's edge. Suddenly, people's heads emerge from steaming pots scattered like pinecones floating in puddles. Drops carve circular patterns in empty pools. I strip and sit on slippery cedar root, soft cushion against my butt. Phoebe follows suit and we plunge into the arms of Mother Earth, catch raindrops on our tongues, talk of finding love. Making our way back from this glory, drenched to the bone, we quick blast the heat in the car, steam up the windows, crank tunes and head for the Port Angeles Laundromat before going back to our soaked site for another two days of this pouring down. Never so warm and content, wearing ponchos, cooking dinner in a downpour, one pot at a time, we make our meal in stages, cuddled up in my newly seam-sealed tent while still light, reading poems to die for.

FIRE IN THE FISHING HOLE

with and for Johnny Olson

At the beginning of the Sunbanks Bass Contest
at Devil's Cove, Steamboat Rock
trucks towing bass boats glisten
as they roll by, become the morning
across Osborn Bay Bridge

Life is this:
loosening up the line
cutting a noose
to let you loose
taking in nine a.m. sun
perched
on a rock staring at
Great Flood Cataclysm
stopped by morning news
on radio

Another peregrine
goes down low on
Russian Olive
branch
shimmering
Kodachrome and sage

Synthesizer
from Banks Lake Blues Fest
vibrates off million-year-old rock face
across Osborn Bay
it thunders Good Morning

Swoosh goes tide
on downed logs

roots and reeds sing
Come on baby, Light my fire…

**

Setting myself on fire
outside Electric City
overcharged on overload
sitting in a mere plastic chair
camped here

Banks Lake herons
Take flight past basalt
next to crows taking off as
a covey *cheep cheeps* in
                    dry brush thickets

We know that rattlesnakes hide in cool dens
          waiting for night to stretch across us

You can call all of this
a swimming hole
if you don't mind
the wetlands sinking you down
in the mud when you
want to crawl in and not dive
it feels like being swallowed whole
like a spear

I am beating off bees making breakfast
in camp for me, John, and Dots
bacon eggs moth-spider omelet?
worms are keeping cool under car in the shade
as we anticipate rolling carp
around our boat

how watching line is
nothing less than a sacred act
we're all waiting for putting the radio
on in the boat casting lines out
listening to them play
Delta Dawn next or maybe
Nirvana

GANESH ON A LEDGE: BIRTHDAY, 2008

for the Radha Yogis on Cedar

Jackson Pollock branches
window canvas Krishna
haiku spider black

Jasper Johns blue curtain,
Divine surrounds Ganesh
like fantasy in Maxfield Parrish
print hidden underneath
a Grecian vase, a pillar, rock
holding up clouds elephant head
extended arms fill the frame

bronze Gauguin orange pumpkin
crowned tusk calls dreams:
another year, new language,
evolving alphabet not yet
spoken, hanging each year
like a trunk,
new sense, new me,
triumphant

I am Pollock branch

Come, birds, land in me
like jet-fuel whitetail streak
soaring West Plains horizon,
passing one leaf at a time,
building on branched bough

Below,
Latah Creek last roe
rainbows
resurrection

MR. TIBBS, WHERE HE IS?

12th and Cedar, Spokane

On the prowl, looking for pets,
Begging, pleading, rolling on his back
His thick fur coats with gravel, stones
Leaves, twigs,
Shit, he don't care
He dons a perpetual tuxedo
Of black and white fur

Mr. Tibbs, where you at?
Where? Where?
They say he slow
That when you look down
Into his yellow eyes
You see nothing but dumb

Bums!

What do they know
About being about
That tall, seeing the world
From a limp curl
Around the three ball
All you'd see
Is yellow too

After all, only three legs
To walk the universe of the block with:
Sadie the dog who snaps
No matter what at drop of hat
Boy holding her back from herself
Over the fence

Mr. Tibbs, you are
More free than me, wandering
Down Adams in the sun
Not walking to work
But walking to everyone,
Everything you want

Not reading any stop signs
not knowing stop but
crying at the bedroom window
to get in
to climb on
to sneak by
to drop down and stretch
show claws
paws up
trust

FUNERAL FOR A COUSIN ON THE SPOKANE REZ

A cold front is coming down from the North
From our neighbor, Alaska.
Today they buried Frankie in frozen Wellpinit dirt.
Up on the Rez, they're always talking death.
You feel the drumbeat: an offbeat heartbeat.

Feeling small is never good unless you are Alice in Wonderland,
And you have lost something tracing steps back.
You feel stolen, displaced.
Colors change, so do dreams
As green becomes greed, a shape.

The basalt flats are mourning to say hello.

Frankie, I am walking stark 1st Avenue
Thinking funerals, and not going to yours.
Walking on a red, I flash on Campbell's Soup,
My cousin, Mary Pat, her mom, Aunt Sis, her cupboard.
That wishing well and donkey on the front lawn,
Doing things we weren't supposed to do
When it got dark.

My body said, go visit my cousin,
Feeling I could learn something
My own family couldn't give me.
Maybe the right to make decisions on my own.

Why I never went to funerals until I was older, I don't know.
I have forgotten who is dead and who is not.
When you haven't seen them dead, they're still alive.
Platonic: The first is not the last.
If I had a kid, I'd name her ItZy Ann.

Is being gone, knowing?
I'm doing wrong and doing it anyway.
If I was celibate, I would be able to keep silent about it.
I fail at being Jesuit anything, even a volunteer,
On the wings of Stephen Dedalus.
I think and feel a protective will that holds onto All.

Watch it drop.
We learn what to wear, how to walk,
And strike matches in the wind.
Our cousins are all around us,
Even when they're not.
It was punks who killed you, Frankie,
In a North Idaho parking lot.
They were kind of like cousins, but not.
More like sneaky twins stealing
the wind from your sails
not racing bikes past you like Heaven
but stabbing you over and over
until it hurts so much you
feel no more pain
and just take it.

SOLEMN PRAISE FOR SOM: September Morning, 2013

for my Buddy, Isamu Jordan

Dear Sleepless, Weightless Som,
I thought I never lived with any regrets.
Today, at 50, I'm full of them.
I knew we'd be left with doubts to overcome.
Took all of what Trucker Dave told me,
You all up Gone.
Was sitting in the SLO Airport,
Rerouted,
Feeling the nest tear away from its song.
All I wanted to say was "*Tell me another one.*"
Yet, that WAS the Tell and
You suddenly had all the answers,
Som.

Today, Spokane will honor you, Man,
As the coaltrains roll through,
And taverns continue to pour.
We keep writing poetry
To overcome downfalls,
Sip coffee, cloud up with the sky
And hell, traffic is a word and it
Will never stop.
People will still
Wash their cars at Brown Bear,
Be homeless, sleep
Under bridges, pull knives,
Cut.

Life will cotinue to hurt like
The best and no matter what,
Many people will die.

Of all of this, I'm certain.
It's what they call wisdom.

Question, Som—
How do we get through the Suffering?
You of all should know.
Knew sellin' your skin
Under the iron of "the man"
With an eye on responsibility,
The paper hitting the door at 4 a.m.
We are now left in the Uprising,
Forming little revolutions
Inside ourselves, and all because of you.

It's up to Us to become our own
Raging inspiration for those
Who can't, hell, won't, show up.
We are pierced with an insatiable hunger,
A swollen need to recover
What's been lost in the Fake Wave
Coming from the Rock Dark
Of this vein of basalt.
You'd think there would be
More mud.

In this wilderness, alone,
I miss your room of words.
Head to the river, the river,
Davis, Craig, Dennis, Dots would say.
I count the many times
The Spokane River whirls
And forms eddies:
Bittersweet, foamy,
And dark as a war.

I tell myself to lend a hand.
Spill out words that might
Mean nothing, kill good taste,
Flip a switch that is
No game in the dark.
You knew that when lights went on
There was a chance
Roaches could race
Across the walls.

Say, what's all this about Time?
It rips from the walls,
Disguises as a stitch saves nine.
Can it actually stand still?
It doesn't matter, does it, Som?
How much of it
Should there be, anyway,
All of it in the world?
Can we ever catch up with it,
Or is that a lie, too?
Like really believing that
Joy kills sorrow. Essence doesn't count.
Everything history and surface has to
Measure up somehow
And mean it.

Just can't find a way, Man, to make days
Longer, have more of it on our hands,
Give me a break!
What about more on our side?
But then, if we did,
How much would it
End up being worth? Who really thought
We'd be paying like we do

For bottled water.
Would we be willing to sacrifice
Dropping the curtain
Way before the call,
Just to take a breather
That never comes?

ON THE BANKS OF LATAH CREEK, VINEGAR FLATS

a love poem for ItZy BitZ

Some enter this world by creek
Become landlocked in it—
The cavernous pits of their dreams.
They come from ancient language
Of the Spokan, basalt canyons,
Deep Rock, why just bleed red?
Some run circles around seasons,
Paint their hooves brown like buffalo,
Maybe white like moon.
All of us are womb of womb,
Born of muscular thunder.
The Great Blue Heron comes
From rapid run…Here he lands!
Hard work, Bird, rock, all one Spirit.
Cold wind makes us happy
Living here in a Firehood of Friends.
Some have ceremony in their bones,
Lullabies:
"*River Run Run…River Run…*
River Run…Run River…"
Winter Spring Summer Fall
I stand inside What I know and
Don't know—Here,
It's like every day is church.
Swimming, swimming round the rocks,
Reindigenizing,
Forever being born
Out of each lost ripple, new one.
Ferns hang down. I know there are no mirrors,
Only depth, the bottom, RUSH,
Survival, shadows in the current.
I still can't see myself!

Only the Past crystallizing
Into Present Myth, sweet food:
Cottonwood, Yarrow, Willow,
This Tepid Earth.
I pray for web, braid my hair,
Think berries/forest/feast,
An old sweet song like
Cherish
Reach down, cradle ItZy
Under my right arm, press her
Soft head body to my heart
And kiss her soft, sweet ear and eye.
Her mouth is black.
We are forever here, my dear,
The Bubba with the Zan.
You are the greatest gift.
You love the water, river.
You chose us, match made natural
By design, just like this creek.
My sweet, smartest girl,
You like the edge, to sniff
With your black olive nose.
How much farther will our journey
Flow, well aware, before we ooze
From reservoirs we've escaped
To edge of creek to river,
To bathe
In its fluid, weightless,
Light Eternal Flow
To ocean and
Beyond.

The Back?
Never back again

And not much in reserve.
Only forward
On and on
You are Me
I am You.

I

DESMET MEETS THE FLATHEAD: 1841

We are an
Invasion, clean to the cut

We are all from
worlds that
are old, eternal

We marry and do not
marry, wear crossed sticks
and cross words

We are the call of the
Rockies, questions peaked cold with hope

We are all good-hearted
safe havens inside ourselves

We spark visions—set up
sacristans hollow as ash

We are sanctuary, rivers
of vestments, beads of stone
sewn sacraments

We share a sense of miracle,
hand signal love affairs,
deconstruct virginity

We are generous, familial,
red that is hunted and bloody

We baptize in gurgling creek,
transport prayers up in smoke of
sweetgrass/sage/frankincense/cobalt

We carry drum, organ, flute,
bones in our pockets, gamble with truth and faith

We play to steal horses, kill one another's authority,
raise angels in brush on the backs of buffalo

We are negotiations for peace
at the end of time no time,
no deadlines, no talk, both heels ground deep
in dirt like bitterroot

ALONG THE OLD HIGHWAY

That time we climbed to 6,000 feet
Where the stars fell over the edge
Of Earth

Standing next to open car doors
We caught echo of ancient buffalo hooves
Stomping across the prairie floor

August wind filled with loose grass
And the ground felt full under our feet
We were part of the blackness

Looking for Orion
That time we passed the constellations
Proclaiming new life in an old breed

As part of this old planet
Our years wrapped our
Sweetgrass tears and somehow

Forever a language born of each other
We are poets whose songs become ribbons
Hung from the moon at welcome

That night the moon in ripples of sweat
Played its drum and expanded

PLAINS FAIR: Late Summer, Montana

with Su

We start the day with beer, drive my truck to first stop
Dixon Store to buy more beer, a six-pack for the road.

The hidden video camera Su carries is rolling, taking
inventory of Mad Dog 20/20 Boones Farm/Thunderbird,

Ditch rot gut they sell to make a buck off a buck.
The Whites who own this reservation store want this shit

to be here. It's an overt way to manipulate
the community by way of a deathly popular commodity.

We cradle cold Buds, rest them between us in the truck.
Tin cans sweat between our thighs. I tell Su to keep

that damn thing rolling as we peel out and away
from abandoned gas pump, leave Dixon in the dust.

Along the Flathead, Highway 200, I confess
about my sex drawer at home, how I always had one,

how it doubles as my underwear drawer. Didn't
everyone have one? Su laughs hysterically,

not knowing what to say as I become Women's
Contemporary History, reveal the very thing

that all women have but don't tell. "What's in there?" she laughs.
"Condoms Gels Dirty Magazines...Hell,

you know what's in there! You have one, don't you?"
She finally breaks down, "Yes!" asks me to explain

this phenomenal essence of what it is to be human.
By the time we get to Plains, we're toasted

over the steering wheel, have found a decent
place to park. We're early. The gates are just opening.

I feel I will be singing, for today is already a song.
We stumble through 4-H stalls lined with rabbits and cows,

listen to the Indian/White Guy comedians
see-saw raw jokes over the intercom as we carouse

pie stands. I choose pecan a la mode to die for.
Drinking makes me ruthless, visible, dynamic,

want a temporary tattoo of a burning Sacred Heart
right here in my cleavage. The tattooer in his stall

is an appeasing, great idea. Su won't stop spouting,
"Wait until Vic sees this!" I want to show the Chief

that I have perpetual guts, that this cowboy fair stuff
brings out the sacrilegious. He can't face things like this.

Will not be seen in indecent company, will not
mingle with the enemy. I want to bring the experience home

to him, trap it in a bottle and transport it back
with fresh footage, showing new times. Is there a point?

Karaoke machines are the rage, novelties at fairs
they charge you to use, provide you with background

music, lyrics all for three bucks. I'm ready, tell Su
"Let's pick out the most rebellious tune." I eyeball

the audience of country toughs: overalled ranchers,
truckers, irrigators on the long haul, women with

brats on both hips singing. I flip through the song sheet,
ask, "How about it?—Dylan's *Positively 4th Street*

How does that one go? Oh, right, got it. Ready. Go."
I sing into their eyes. I sing the minstrel's words

to live by. Six stanzas. It never ends, that's the point.
We're trapped in the eternal thrust, pushing its way out,

a day needing a nightcap at PairADice Bar.
Paradise on the rocks, just for one day.

FLYING OVER EVARO

during "Trickster" rehearsals

Huey Lewis says "*Goodbye*"
in Missoula airport,
"*Thanks for the drink*"
I hug him in his stiff leather tour jacket,
grip his woolen arm,
simply say "*Good Luck*"

On board the flight
the moon is oozing warm soy
over Lake Missoula
rattlesnake bottom

No more stories about us,
only trickster within us
coming out in the form of plays
written, cast, produced,
performed

We glide down ancient corridors
cut in dirt, yellow tunnels, ravines,
little housetops,
ranches in a row,
fence encircling fence
(strange domino effect)
on swollen hills like
puffed breasts of
soft brown ducks

Shadows carry windsong
under our wings:
sunset pink Easter snow
powders thistleheads below,
standing firm in dark ridge ravel

before us, hot mountain
melts like Icarus
in flight

PATTEE CANYON

"We're all heirs, waiting for this moment."

This is huckleberry country, Vic says.
Missoula dogcry echoes canyon,
chipmunk clings chirping discontent
while Vic reads from old journals,
face stroked by ponderosa
shadow lace, leaving the heart
of the matter, what matters is Fall.

Equinox moonrise: clear air up here,
down below is firechoke across
Missoula Valley floor.

Great Grandson of
Little Grizzly Bear Claw
flips papers with his paw
at the picnic table,
Yogi Bear serving dog
mustard memories
under pine butter.

It is soft September,
soft as Aunt Marie's night light
Toledo, Ohio, the summer I stayed
cradled in quad sixes.

Weather and Chief take me back
To dreams of six, transfixed.

PATTEE CANYON REVISITED

The road is closed
so we park and walk in.
Suddenly, we think we may have
lost the stash—
Out an overstuffed pocket?
Gas station? Curb at the Pump?
Old Timer's? Le Petit Outre?
Pattee Canyon? Anywhere else
we were, could be there, on the ground—

Maybe someone already discovered
they were winners of a pickpot,
turning the container over,
seeing "If lost, return to X..."
written on the back,
making them feel guilty,
knowing someone else
once owned it and it
isn't just up for grabs.

GRAVEL FOR SALE

on White Coyote
Road they sell
gravel off piles
at foothills of mountains
lightning on
gold—like horizon
bone hid tight in canyon
rare rubble: classified
bought and sold
limestone rumble—
yellow wild rose
pop plump petal
sunset howling
down logs
crossed

THE MYSTICAL CAPPUCINO

My barista
Is a curly-swoop
Red-headed soft
Spoken priest
Who hears confessions
5-7 a.m. daily
I order a triple
Soy cappucino
He wipes and steams
And cleans the wand
In the tray of
The machine
As ground beans
Slightly cocoa cinnamon
Children nymphs
Of the butterflies sing
Dank day
Glad I'm not skiing
Says Scarecrow
Pumpkinhead who has
A cornrow shape cut out
On the worn
Wooden counter
She is in layers:
Tattoos piercings
Large hole in her nose
She shifts exposing
The long length of her calf
Harlequin stockings
Double slip Her hair is
Lime-yellow with blonde wings
I can describe her

As she swirls
In circles around her chair
Explaining the season, a smell,
The Autumnal Moon is
Hovering in Aries: Communication
If anybody is listening!
My barista shakes the
Soy over dark shots
makes sprigs of foam
This is a mystical cappucino
I feel it
Pixie Boy collecting dishes
Tossles his hair and slaps
His flag cloth against his
Straight thin leg
Taps his pointy-toed shoe
Gingersnaps They're good today
I smile at all the small asses
With a poof of their
Biscotti wands
They take a bow
And send you off,
Charged up

ITZY AFTER RAVENWOODS

for Todd and Kate

ItZy smells like Jewel Basin cabin
place of birth and rebirth
stove smoke
sweetgrass prayers up

Damp kettle steam
a trace of huckleberry musk,
if I brush her tail
the scent of dry pine escapes

ItZy when I rub her
sheds split wood chips
wet forest needles
the bottoms
of her paws are smooth
river stones

ItZy's hair is soft
as cedar moss in steady rain
we made a path across

Surely she absorbed
some leather and wool
and her heart beats low
gentle, as a star's glow
in the open dark

The way you've
taught me,
we want that,
and the rest of your forest
to get lost in

II

SALMON = DAMN

Salmon are extreme and exceptional swimmers
Sad they have to careen against ladders,
overcome dam obstacles, concrete walls.
If they could, who or what would they bomb?
All they seek is Homeland
through channeled scablands,
thick with sagebrush and basalt.

The Quinault, Chinook, Coeur d'Alene, Spokane,
Yakama, Nez Perce, Umatilla, Warm Springs,
they all know the struggle,
having to stroke against the current
that seeks to overpower them,
barricade them into extinction
as they make a desperate attempt
to cycle from ocean to freshwater, back again.

Today, you can't think salmon without thinking DAM.
What will it take to shake
the manmade powers
out of their own tangled nets?
Enough with the targets/threats of being caught.
So full of guilt and regret that turns sour
(into more power).

It's a sick cycle circling back
that ignores the fact that salmon
are the True Leaders,
defenders, barometric symbols
of sustenance, freedoms,
rights we can't take for granted or neglect
(even the very waters
drying up and away).

Their appearance speaks
what is right and working.
If they are suffering, we, too, suffer.

CUT THE ROPE

Twinkle, twinkle little star.
It's only 12 degrees.

It was a taut skin
I found myself in,
a tight old plight
wrapped around myself.

I played,
we played, a Pentagon.
Wrong?

There was no wrong
to being toss of a bone with
no catch.

Pulled the rope taut.
Reached behind,
pulled a sharp knife,
hidden all right
in case of dark nights
like this.

So I hold tight
to blade, the knife,
my own hand,
slide and shred
the braided rope
from around me
so profoundly,

make Houdini like me.

THE KEY

After ten years together it's only his copy of the apartment key left in the empty mailbox simply clipped to a direct mail postcard by a worn out clothespin. No note no words no say no nothing says everything. It's a somber plunge, this huge Gone-for-Good. I squeeze what's left in my palm—imagine his touch in my fingers rubbing the grooves, my heart drenched in cold metal love. He kept his Own Self close to his chest, a warm mature pocket opens new doors. I look up at the sky, swimming pink salmon sky—a wide cloud stretch of bed burning up from under us.

THE END

death is hidden
in the heat of fire
the first level chakra
muladhara

begin
and
separate illusion
from desire
choose a new sex
path   ride a wave
of salt

fridge full
of leftovers after leftovers
food we can't stomach
what we ourselves
can't fill
of each
other

holiday ham
salted
heartbreak
cured

DAD'S BUICK

How many
White
1991
Buick Centuries
Are
In
Spokane
Anyway?

How many
Times
Will I
Turn
Quick
Thinking
It's you
Driving by?

How many
Roads
Can I
Wear down
Before
There's
No tread?

Plastic
Scorpions
From Arizona
Glued
To the dash—
They come
Alive and sting.

How many
Red heart
Stickers
Remain
On your
Steering
Column?

Head bobbing
Bulldog shattered
German Shepherd
Must sit in back
Before they
Break neck.

How many
Visits
With warranty
In hand
Does it take
To fix the damned brakes?

How many
Miles
Will you put
On
Dad's Buick
Now
That we're
Not together?

How many
Days
Will it take

For me to forget
What dirty laundry's
Left in the trunk?

How many
Mistakes
Must I make
Before I realize
I am wrong?

Valley streets
Will curve along
Knowing
Better than ever could
Dad's Buick.

FALLEN EMPIRE

force
separates us
from our words
an affair of
hidden feelings
we cheat
each other
out of pit
of patience

we are at wits' end
with our world
in ruins
cause heart-suffer hurt

hard to talk
Truth
when we go
on blowing
evenings up
in the dark

harvest salt
from our eyes:
coarse pillars
engulfed in smoke
coiled snake
takes stabs
at the Caesar
within.

THE TERRORIST AT THE DUKE: 3rd & Cannon, Spokane, WA

I watched someone (the
way I used to)
be a human doorbell,
at the Duke,
from our old Apartment F,
pull a curtain back,
slide the window over,
three floors up,
hang the ledge,
toss a key down
to let
someone up.

Now I don't live there.
Now, past mounds of snow,
I merely watch,
this early March,
a terrorist of my past,
recalling the way it was
to live there when I did,
and how it was,
the way it is now,
wanting to blow
it up.

Being a terrorist of the past
requires: all that matters
is NOW, not THEN.
I get it serious in
my head:
I made a choice,

I am the sum.
I felt it, plotted,
then destroyed it.

Memory, like an old visitor,
lets anything in.
The sadder, the better.

As a focused purist,
I am careful what I let flow,
what I surrender to,
what I strap across my chest,

what I let BLOW.

SALMON LOVE

for Jimmy Leroy Dotson

I was in love with a salmon once It happened on the ocean on a bobbing boat 15 miles off the Vancouver Island coast My boyfriend Dots was even there but I didn't care My emotions got the best of me The swells were grey and rough slapping up the sides of the craft I had him on a hook as fast as lightning strikes My rod electric as I grabbed it What a dramatic commitment Like diving in Like a long night of drinking without drinking Just hanging in there with irrational obsession No turning back Hold on and get ready for the Chase It was all my fault I didn't know he was Coho or how big he was until he broke through the hazy glass abyss and surfaced twisting surrounded by waves he made up around himself What a dancer over the ocean top Tipping on his wide tail Trying to get off He put up a good fight the way love affairs plunge fast He dove headfirst back down into the Deep as Dots Dick Captain Charlie yelled *Let your line out Let 'er out You got this Zannnnnie* I have never been cheered on as I fell hard in love In fact most people I know ignore you once you're entranced and drowning in that sensual pool Don't blame them Heartstrings kidnapped Not all there Just not yourself Damn it It's hard to be present when your mind is a sopping love trap Here..... This....was only a mere 50 pound line fed out between us No promises No guarantees you'll survive falling in love In the struggle I felt this is not just a fish He's a helluva lot more than that He's history on a hook Think the odds you ever succeed landing anything out here in this vast wilderness sea For hours of bore all my line did was sing like a mythical mermaid Then suddenly BAM It all became a test of time and massive muscular grip Drumming up all you got inside to take the Ancient Marvel on What a handsome proposition: giving him more line, the tease such a contradiction: giving him more freedom more space to ultimately arch my rod and wait for him to run himself down *You wanna tire him out* Dick groaned *Until he eventually surrenders* How SAD to think What a way to ACT I wasn't brought up this way

Loving on a line hurts The resistance can last hours It is a Bitter End Exhausting Humbling Will he get it up? Will I get him up? It could all be for naught But that's the chance one takes Love Affairs/Never Lasting Throbs Then Dick Dots Captain Charlie Bug and Dwight surround me Call out *Bring him in Bring him in You got him You got him* I almost just want to let him Let it all go Give up Why? Guilt A sense of greed That sinking feeling it's all about me and pleasure What an asshole What a jerk to lure him from the ocean like this Steal his life just to eat him up What am I thinking? What feels right? And right then Dots leans over the side with the net and pulls him up and in He flops and knocks hard against my legs He probably wants to take me down with him Dick says *Grab him up* He's a Brisbois (Indian) He knows what it's like to pray and take at the same time everything wrapped up in offerings gratitude survival rushing all at once from your lips and limbs I reach down and out with my hands Wrap him in my arms He slips out I grab him again Hug him up hard and close Silver scales smear across my chest I hold him for dear life I hold him hard Tell him I'm sorry Kiss him all over and I do it I love him to death

III

BREAKFAST IN HONOR OF TOM

for Tom Davis

Get close to river's edge
without falling in—
tether
on the edge,
what's to lose?

I choose Central Foods
figure a stiff one (couple)
grab a baguette from the basket,
say hello to the staff,
sit at the bar, alone,
get buzzed, even.

Wearing a black derby
I remember Davis' obsession with
"Playboy of the Western World"
how Irish we both were
without rehearsal
deep in our being, our voices
bunched over.
I order an Irish coffee.

You taught me what
was okay to be sorry for,
that not everything is worth
an apology, no matter
how hard you try.

Don't feel you have to
squander everything, even if
it feels right, even if you feel
completely out of your wits,
drowning, rock tied to your waist.

Know your own fucked-up self,
embrace it, honor, proclaim it,
mostly through poetry. Do it.
Do it until you die. That's
advice Tom would lend
on an offbeat day when rain fell hard
on Spokane low river
swelled, grass smelling pussy rich.

He'd say the crows are
doing a dance, their spirits
cawing out.
Listen, and you, too
will not be afraid
to die, ever.

STORMY BALLYCONNELL SUNDAY

for Dermot Healy and Helen

Awake from nap on seaside cot staring at the wall, bare light bulb dangles white on white, Benbulben Imagination, close yet so far. NOON bell rings "Angelus" and Mercy fills the room in the shape of a blue worn door. Come in, Angels, please! Paper carp swims overhead in humble writing room, a mobius strip of smoky half thoughts. *Trivial Pursuit* waits in neglect for the Resurrection of Gaelic. I roll over, on the floor, and yawn. Too much Cavalry Cabernet last night, was called "one gone Indian" wrapped tight in blanket-papoose so I wouldn't fall out. It's a wet Sunday morning crack in the door, lamb on the broil, mint jelly, misty sparkle of a green glass bowl, ocean aglow on the table/out the window. That's Helen playing teacups in her kitchen clanging octaves of ceramic medicine. Outside, the West Irish Coast Atlantic sprays rock jetties cut with boozy air: periwinkle cling to what once felt solid. Somewhere, crow digs its hole, filly finds shelter in its stall, lace curtains close up torn from Trouble more diligent than coming storm.

ROCKY ROAD TO DUBLIN

In Allihies
where mist and snow have names
that make wrecks on rocks,
sun becomes a discussion
about what just happened,
a magic trick in several sessions
of rain-washed love

Repeat the road to Trinity Square:
you, walking on a rose shoulder

My dorm room
one big corner off the square,
building thirty, first floor, number twelve

The Registrar thought I was
Mr. Zan Agzigian,
a crippled old Armenian scholar
with no need for condoms

We christen that room
looking out on the campanile,
glimmering tennis court,
a bouquet of balled
carnations at our feet,
four pears bought at open market:
communion

Down Temple Bar
Italian Dublin-style
it's pasta I ask you to order

over a bottle we rekindle
goatwalk sharp rocks of Allihies,
canvases in daffodil-filled studio,
the continuous rapture of the
schoolhouse vortex that made us numb
to deadlines:
how many times did we miss the draw?

Never

Now we're ten minutes late
for the First Act at the Abbey:
exuberant unabashed full of wrenched
gliding gutwords
drenched in marvelous seasalt

THE BAR

for Dave Caffrey

Into this bar we walk. I figure he'll have a cigar by tomorrow.
I light my own. Wait. Tomorrow might never walk in,
but we'll see. I'm patient, not worrying, thinking just another dream.

I can take this rockless floor so close to salty ravaged shore,
pencil-thin trail to goat cave, tucked in touch of town glow.

Can we fake rapture when ocean rain falls hard?
The rush from the rear is coming: a gale, massive swirl,
across hair of island. Two ticket ton.

You roll in, magic, a wirehot moon,
corner of the doorway framed by trees.
The trees are lonely, so to me,
flowered patron,
I like flowers, your friend, this walk,
that sweater, what's on that telly,
the way you order
another shot.

THE BUS OUT OF GALWAY: Summer 1995

A crow digs a hole at the side of the road
A newborn filly has the hill
The 4th hole on the golf course
Has a red flag flying and so does
The Red Tag Petrol
A sold house and another sold house
Look dead as two men stand on a corner
Round sweater-bellied and smoking
At the stop light we pull up and stop
In front of a sun-worn window
Cluttered with teetering tins of beer
As the bus takes a turn a man with a cap
Steps outside a laundromat
Behind him sheets are spinning spinning
A fag hangs loose from his lips
Then the smell of burning tar
A roller approaches the bus
As a boy wearing red chases our wheels
Someone is leaning up against a shed
During one of our stops two boys
On a bench are eating ice My mother likes
To eat ice We are waiting in the depot
Someone's sipping soda He presses
His hand to his chest Wait, what's that?
His hand is holding the fence
A clover board sways against a
Galway windy sky The pub even has
Lace curtains And here comes the driver
Bouncing back into his seat with the radio on
The Angelus Noon Bells ring There is
A threat of a postal strike and
The last thing we see pulling out

Is a blue worn door that has white smoke disappearing
Through the top into white skylight

Another summer, click, click, clicks
I see a long rock wall The bus speeds up
It makes me think those rocks
My last night in the Bay
Something about a church with
No windows A No Dumping sign
Lamb was my last supper
I missed Mick Jagger and Charlie Watts
By that much at the White Rabbit
Across the aisle a man
Is alone with his ways Maybe he's dreaming
Of the kettle and that next cuppa tay
The sun is risen and glistening
And cuts through trees between buildings
Flinting across glass as we turn out
The driver turns the radio on and it plays
The Beatles' "Get Back"
Driver asks, "Anyone mind?"
And all I can think of is
"When will I get back
To Ireland?"

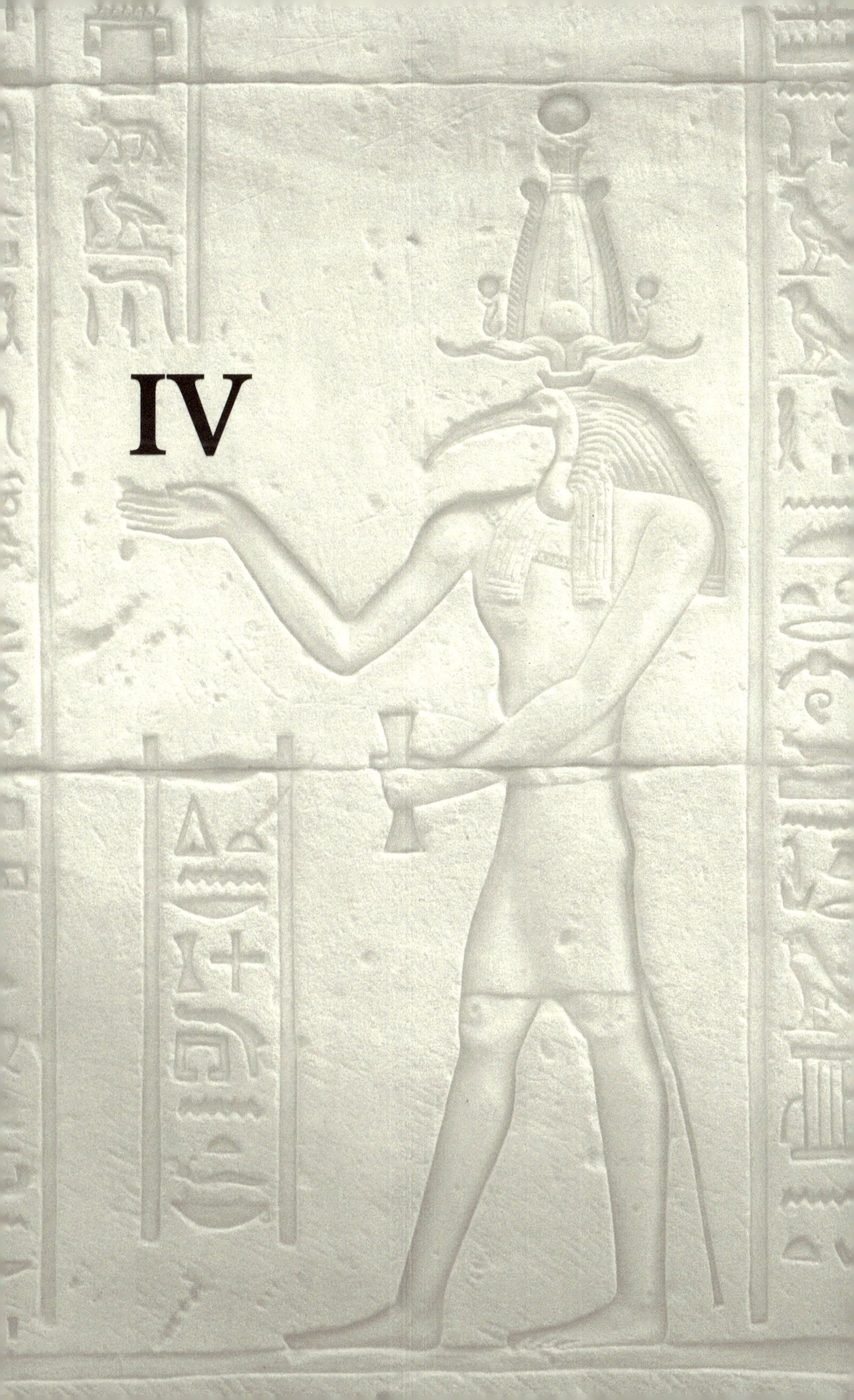
IV

GOOD REASON RESERVOIR DITTY

How many breaths
Does it take to deep dive?
How many regrets to edge over a cliff?
How dark is the night
When you're always up in it?
How little we know
The deeper we go
The slower our hearts beat
The quicker we drop
You have to find
A good reason
To rise
With reserves
To the top
'Cause it's
Nothing until
You want it
When you want it
Then you get it
Until you lose it
Or time drains
Us of it
That is love

HAIL MARY, FULL OF GRACE

for Mary Pat O'Donnell

Hail Mary, Full of Grace,
You are so full of earth.
Blessings on you. You are so woman.
Your fruits and vegetables are most welcome.
They come from the womb of dirt.

Jesus, what you do is holy.
Hey there, Mary, Mother of Sons,
Smudge us with sage
Now until the Hour
Of our Mother's death,
A-ho

TRELLISES

for Todd, ND

A flight of your favorite jazz
spins soft silk through warm February dusk
as I gracefully unfurl each knot you have tied
around secured trellises love
has unloaded on me—

These knots make me think of each embryo
you have guided into this world,
each knot of tension you have had a hand in
unraveling with gentility and grace—

As fumbling student of this world's
bumps and waves, my tender fingers keep
me further and further from rebirth, try and re-try
to draw a map of each step it took to wrap,
rope over and over, under what your skill has left—

The wrought iron arches are easy to lift,
go overhead in a shifting glide like hope,
where they are laid to rest in a purposeful, diligent
pattern against old cedar fence
in an even line, forming a smooth billow across the sky,
I look up and at them—
it is déjà vu—I have been here before, alone, trapped
in a similar dream of loss—maybe several dreams,
one after another, where each scenario is
a mere blink in the eye of survival—

The holy dark stepping back unfolds a symphony
of vision: constraint, withdrawal, reaching out from fear,
a feeling that with each step back comes a release,
a letting go of all I ever thought I knew, unknown—

A lone star above breaks open in its brightness,
and I break, my heart, my soul, in two,
perhaps even more—for two seems like not enough:
Black white Right wrong
Good bad Sorrow laughter,
Psalm, the ancient song
I'm left of You

PRAYER TO THE BOMB

full of Radical Forgiveness

Please, Dear Bomb,
don't go off,
at least, not now,
how about
not even
right away,
never, maybe.

I envy you. You can detonate.
(Then again, who can't?)
You get
the bad rap
and handle it
well, in fact,
better than any other
weapon.

Forgive us for everything.
Want to trade some
brass for white scarves?
Bullets for white gloves?
You are worth *any*thing
and *every*thing I have to offer.
You are a part of my life.
I love you,
Dear Bomb.

You are my friend.
I'll treat you right as long
as you forgive me for
it *all*. Your power is

almighty, ubiquitous,
I get that, always
focused
on a target.
You are something
glorious and holy,
dare I say sacred.
Let me hold you close
before you take off,
implode, explode,
detonate, scatter, shatter,

~~drop~~.

It's the least I can do
with what I've come to
know
yet still don't
understand.
Wasn't Oppenheimer wrong?
Aren't you really a
bully by design?
Or is this all talk asking
you to just be safe
for now?

I respect your unpredictable
ways more than how much
my neighbor mows his lawn.
I can work through rust
like anybody's
business to get
to the heart of the matter.
But the matter is,

would you please not
make any decisions
right now?

Be still
Breathe
Reconsider

again
and
again

maybe
for a
very
long
time

perhaps,,,,,

,,,

,,,

, , ,

,

,

forever.

PILGRIMAGE TO TURNBULL

In this unsettled heat of Self,
Struggling to dampen the cloak of death,
It's migratory to park here, get out
Without map and tender into
This unlikely paradise, a raptor's refuge.

Having a dog so small with me
That an owl or hawk or coyote
Could pluck off into eternity—
My soul murmurs, "Spare her and
Let it be me..."
But I have already been plucked
From this earth.

Choristers rise from teeming boundaries
As I'm careful not to hinder
Illuminating sunbeams that burst onto
An outcrop of basalt (my tumult).

I stumble, instead, around my own shadow:
Sorrow elongated/exaggerated/exhausted.
ItZy, my oracle, stops and turns to make sure
I am still visible in my invisibility.
It is hard to fake out your own shadow.

The strain of Cheney wind, in a fine balance
Between winter and spring, always so big
And out in the open with its unpredictability,
Mimics the climb of a little frog hidden
And rustling in dry broom
Of dormant grass. It tangles up its leap,
Arid and sustained, in its return to receded pond
That lies flat and brown as a buckwheat pancake.

Thick in the drown of an underworld,
I'm dreaming time to Sigur Ros,
Envisioning an Icelandic orchestra like them
Of Northern Lights flashing across this stage
Of gusto singing a birdsong to wrestle myself back
To timbered, articulate spirit.
I'm certain this expanse holds unforgotten notes
I have to forget to remember again.

At the edge of a wooden foot bridge, ItZy bombdives
A cascading wall of cattails, revealing a plump of canvasbacks.

It is barren here with no one else appearing. Those who
Don't know better would call this nothing. They are afraid
Of wildness, full of ancient direction, flights of
Education. I am a student of this room imploring
The eagles, the red-tails for my wings back. I've got
To beg from something, place cold fingers in
Numb pockets. My psyche is a cryogenic biome
Preventing me from burning up in flames.

Down the sodden service road I hear the calls
Of old ways. Nothing in this everythingness
Is out of place. I am in the eternal now,
Seeping through the fine grain of cataclysmic ecstasy
Of day. Craig, old friend, departed Bickerton, floods
In through a narrow canyon of recall, pulling rank
Past Archangel Norvel (how does a spirit do that?)
Bick was always the first to proclaim Equinox
Like BINGO to dull-witted dark pitted Spokane barbacks
Sloshing in the suds – BUTTERCUPS! he'd yell as they feasted
Their eyes on their own ache of channeled scablands:
Sharp-pointed insides created by volcanic thrust.

Ponderosas bent, we walk near breaking—my stories
Afoot, tenuous mercies recollecting everywhere's
A grave, and anytime we can die, and do.
Nature breaks this news to us as a beatific vision.
I tell myself, to an unconvincing sky, that I'm hospitable,
Prayerful with each step in and out of mud-grooved
Mind. I welcome the song of trumpet swans overhead,
The exquisite breeze they spread from the flap of
Their wings, like palms together in immaculate manner.
As feathers, each finger lines up against the next
To next, a winging of spirit reborn to return
Again and again, mating for New Life.

RIVERSONG

for Tom Davis

Four geese fly upstream
as I stack dry rocks
mumble wet words—
toss snowballs into
current, watch
them melt as I wash
sorrow out my
cold hands in
rolling river water, channel
cool winter away
through
sun's blue day rays

I place a photo of you I took
in soggy gravel, it takes off and floats,
gets caught up in a round batch
of red willow reeds
sticking up and out, tied to the current,
your image gets drenched, then drowned,
resurfaces torn to pieces,
ripped up and
bobbing
peaceably
down like pieces
of waffle coated in syrup

All is at rest,
even this restless
heart soaking
sand on shore with
dirt rough laughter
spinning sparrow

flutters up from my throat
twisting beats in lines
to make sense
I step into current
all at once enter
this rapid dream
not wanting
to step back

MY BREATH ON THE WINDOW

for Korrine

My reflection
in the wet dew:
Do I dream
that I know I am?
I think
I live here
somewhere
through the pane
without breaking

Lawns,
the west horizon
boxcar line
clinging like hope
to creek cliff's edge
on arrival/pause

Coeur d'Alene
dewdrops
fake teardrops
dripping
off branches
as the sun falls
over fences,
a green garage

Ponderosa light
a rose silhouette
of bird as it soars slight
as petal fallen
from bloom
stem
to wintry ground

THIS BLESSED STATE

for Diana der Hovanessian

It is a blessing to sit quiet
In a restaurant and not talk—
To think nothing but
The sky, trees, the sun,
To be alone sipping coffee
With ancient Armenian poetry
Staring for an instant
At a parking lot and watching
A car pull out.

To know where I am, and how I got here
To pray to the dead I remember
In a moment's swallow of hot milk
To feel the tears well up—Imagining
Vibrant Constantinople, the artistry of
Thir, Nareg, Frik. Blouze, Kouchag, Nova
falling into the hands of Ottomans.

Sitting in this tingling sorrow, I am
a crevice in clay.
Here in Spokane, I sip Vietnamese soup—
Remember the French: the invaders: the Turks
Wonder how the Montana Freemen
Ever make a point with gun rhetoric—
Doubt whether we are ever free.
It is a blessing to sit quiet and not talk—
To not be coerced into spelling Yahweh,
forced into rebirth.

BEAR LANGUAGE

Once Upon Our Time, a deep switch at humanity's core somehow decided to target BEARS Since then this obsession has conjured up long-lasting love-hate feelings Eventually BEARS rebelled they broke into apartments got into garbage fell from trees downtown against their will tranquilized hiked through city parks ransacking vehicles got trapped in vans of trouble wandered in and out of places until snow flew We started blaming so much on them that *Grizzly* became an easy kill-off word Suddenly no federal protection no preservation just the thoughts of them being in the way of sagebrush prairies berries plump bugs tree bark reoccupying history out from the den over swiftly melting glaciers scarce huckleberries down to a trickle cold creek beds no real service to chokecherries Now a threat to the heart of even salmon BEARS are some new urban elephant public dynamite We're no real fans of their backyard antics tracking resort decks storming coops making a hobby of garbage compost bins Tearing through window screens doors raiding birdseed suet fast food trashcans Going wild in zoos These are not bright ideas But all the same we expect to trap them make them disappear They ain't no rabbits in hats They'll just rise back up Make no mistake: leave your Missoula garage door open and see what happens! SURPRISE Trouble Holy Terror BLACK BEARS bite necks throats provoke campers Just put out dog food litter canned goods No wonder BEARS bite through tents have cultivated inherent problems get captured killed Don't mix BEARS with advocacy They deserve better than us stealing their corridors food habitat It's out of touch to think just tents and backpacks us sleeping on the ground will keep them from approaching us without incident They can smell a hick from out of state from miles away and know the name of THAT tune We just keep building bigger ranch houses hang bird feeders in the wilderness make city slickers out of chickens

What a TEASE We just don't innovate develop think smarter or past compressed plastic for hassle-free pickup In fact we are doing nothing to discourage BEARS from moving farther into town BEARS may be even better than us at tracking and reporting humans' whereabouts BEARS may even be filing reports on us anonymously *She (that bitch) can make me 568 cookies I'd still eat her willy-nilly* BEARS don't like coaxing or pipelines! What the hell BEARS don't like walls! They don't confuse fatality with finality *Ever hear the word co-exist (not electrical fence)?* Technology aside isotopes and genotypes lie We call them names in our so-called reports: with our hot-shot new-wave monitoring systems population trends geological surveys GPS tracking collars We say all that shit all to better understand how BEARS tick Oh no we are in the DARK still allowing hunts as BEARS hold counsel under apple trees like jam down peoples' throats for good reason: Store more trash more garbage Just try to make BEARS more human-like with donuts hot dogs If only they would listen to some *jazzzzzzz* smoke joints chant *om* Sit still learn to curb their anger through yoga and mindfulness we'd probably even call THAT ancestral

BOWIE DAWN

gray dawn forlorn
wake up slow creep
and i and it yawn and peak

a beckon call o'er bitter bluff
i bow to East cinnamon sweet
and it is *Oh You Pretty Thing!*
i pray my soul to yours i keep

from bone of creek come notes
each roll a current soon awakes
each tune a joint like sand it slips
and sinks one down all that more deep

to counteract
the truth that grief gives us a gift

it's oh so hard to trust this grasp
until we drink our coffee black
remove that ring we won't take off
until we see the bottom cup us
in its grip and bite us back

departed now you lean in Light
a Superstreak Be One w/ Bright
the sky is ripped in pink/blue half

i draw a blank my dog a blanket
this morning is androgynous
the way the news does not commit
to this or that
to me it is neutral, flat

this odyssey of sacred flight
is cold cold wind from south palouse
it shakes the heads: last summer's sun-
dry flowers bend all brittle brown

reminders still
of summer's drought leaving skulls for beds
they tremble brisk outside my pane

i see through them and that old game
where suffering has name-no-name
no place or home a beggar's hand

my garden box: dry zinnias no color
seeds re-seed no less and even though
what i see now is chunks of snow
like lunar rock surrounding heart brisk
early mourn

i just can't wait 'til i am born
to play awake when i am hearth
half-truth amid these barren
words performed

TULIP IS A PLACE

Magnolias sent down
flying tongues,
in one crush, streaks of brown
on the arboretum lawn
a sheet as silent as
the parting lick
on the curve
of a vulva
glistening half-moon
wet skinned
day being born before me
dawn in rewind

Going going
I've been all night
unfolding dropping
myself off at home inside
each time I think of what
was Not

To the ground
I did not drop,
did not succumb
to sucking cock,
taking it in or up

There was no love lost on me,
lifeless lottery,
it was no random give and take
date, did not displace
any part of me, even though
I suffer from severe drought

I comb this lawn
to the point of orgasm
seeded not in haste
or disciplined rows
but cultivar
filled with self-preservation
of character

Nothing
but firm Heirloom
clutched in my
blossoming
bosom

CLOUDS*CONTRITION*YARN

CLOUDS What you say up there, Big Weather—? I'm in awe of what You pin to Spokane worn frozen as a widow's peak on Adams—South Hill backlit and cornered In no other place on Earth but here your pillowy breath lays blankets over my own Big Blue Boo-Hoo

CONTRITION Our lives are steep long slopes cut deep by faults fissures erosions leaving shallow soil rocky surfaces exposed

YARN *for Jacob Hunter* We are buttons shells invincible latches broken glass neon in rooms strung up with twine in mirrored pearls We are stories put in scrapbooks Buddhas on a sill and orange-scented tic-tacs We are rolled-out carpets walked on geysers sprung with cedarjuniperpine cottonwood sage tumbleweed limestone We are starfish seahorse seaweed urchins woven A short stretch of yarn in your mother's womb

STANDING ON DUNGENESS SPIT

Sea lions bob like balding old men.
Gray heads tangle in ocean white foam.
We bow at this mystical passage
where Dungeness River empties into
Juan de Fuca's mouth
surrounded by graveyard spit
from campsite to shoreline to mountain.

We bob through life like seals: balding clear-cut hills,
chart geometric territory to memory.
What harm could come, Isosceles?
Tide, we're stranded.
We wade wearing masks of wet rain.
Our bones in our legs drift and float,
pebbles ring through clavicle.
Horizon rolls flat, into fragments,
spits us out, lets go,
we resurrect.

LOVE

It's outcome bring down come around on and on off the cuff
tough viral vital violent far away close too close lost toast indigo
better worse gone done wrong stoned ruined rude revelatory sorry
boring lurid sexy meaty

greedy needy seedy expensive poor naked raw sweet sour power
crass rash pressed messed with messed up broken whole in pieces
grateful graced blessed confessed moody borrowed stolen golden
rotten forgotten habit hard wrapped stacked racked wicked mystic
religious mantra mudra muddy funny craved believed innocent
babies crumbled tumbled ridden driven coaxed

cinnamon leather underwear deadly volatile waxing waning
moonbeams sunshine mortal immortal dead dismal terrible
horrible trouble bubbles smoky choked stumbling rattled red-
hearted melting boiling frozen icy dicey mousy loud silent
whispered nothing something insurmountable quizzical curious
furious enriched spinning sinking quicksand

echoed bargained tried hidden secrets tricks walled full of holes
smudged smug hugs

was'ndwasn'ts sunken treasured measured weathered tested fruity
wise bold old told storied improbable sheepish dishonest trusted

fussy crusty fresh encased dark caved crashed burned buried
hurried harried hurtful betrayed sunbeams rust a bust an issue
traditional retentive attentive Love—it's few if not all of these
things a little or less or more or less some of them give or take one
or two

SAD SNOW

for Brian Schuman

Virgin Mary
Mother Snow
Undulating
Gray sheet sky

Dry compact
Snowflakes
Snowball
Snowman
Snow mounds

Leaning under streetlight halos
Hosanna high
Into each other
Snuggled up
Against car tires

Hubcap high snow
Run out of gas snow
Miss your brother
Sister, ways you used to
Play in it when you
Were small snow

Cocoa hot sweet sadness
Taste it numb
On the tip of your tongue
Tearflakes
Frozen words inside like ice

The meltdown
Covering all of who
You are, the years, my friend
Melting in a shroud of kindred cold
Saying it's okay
To let you go snow

A DEEP NEW YORK DREAM

a world's record sent me here
a chance to send all of me measured
in milliseconds
so here i am

there is a time
like tonight when phones
are still ringing in subways
no one is answering but
dreams are still
dreamt

no one remembers these dreams
fit me in the jar before you pour
squeeze me in a sweater
yearn for a table by the window
fingerprints on the wine glass
nitelite violent femmes
a howard johnson's peppermint ice cream
coneyisland hot dog

ALICE
to go

without a doubt i would stay in the city all (nite)
even if it meant going back
to bad habits from the beginning
brite (lites)
smoking and drinking
on until dawn
with trash collectors
running down
43rd and 9th

no foolish deed done in dark
was in need
of analysis
research
or thought
putting hats on we took hats off

we tried this makeup
other stuff you said smashing Cuban
down 23rd Lower Chelsea
i believed you
after *monkey*

tonight i drank the D--
wanted off needed to get myself
back to a time when i never questioned
anything but questioned everything
at once

glad
the blowup you had with her
was with her and not me
i understand but need nothing more
to go on

MIRACULOUS

for Sebastian and Chelsea

on Main I meet
a magical miracle
in the arms
of father wearing
rainbow knit cocoon
for and on
around him

mother arms
by mother I mean
Full Circle
back from edge
of river Five/Six days old
along ancient bank
of PEACEFUL VALLEY
world

came pink a 10
on a scale of 1-10
scarlet star poem

lives yet to be written
together
in this new sink

ROCK
          set in
ROCK
atop
ROCK
is ROCK

HOME Indian Laurel sun
this hole in time

BLESSED SIDEWALK

MORNING WALK TO WORK

for Jan Quintrall

Misty train graffitied on every car
cuts through cold bluesky morning
                              cold steel blue on blue ahead
                                cold glistening shards
                                        cool shattered blue glass
                                        spread across the sidewalk
                              littering the Railway Alley underpass

early winter morning wet
I am hazy as weather without coffee
Someone took a blue glass bottle
of fancy water whatever whatnot
reached back and smashed against the wall
of buttressed concrete
leaving a collage a blurry Polaroid
undetected

Ice cold Pacific PacMan
bursts through plastic flaps
for doors
in shorts wool socks & boots
with a trashcan brimming
with fresh shaved ice
tonnage he ejects tipped curbside
slush-slush   offthedolly
leaving crystal snowcone mounds
along the curb piles
                              of fresh pure cool

cradled by blue cold clickety-clack clickety-clack
                                        clickety-clack clickety-clack

Trains cross tracks overhead
            pigeon disturbed
finch puffed swoop dart above
below a scattering of spent butts
by parking meter pole newspaper wet
on the step   Might be the first in
might have to make the first pot

maybe ItZy will run down the hallway
dance to see me   pound code*code*code*code*
clickety-clack clickety-clack   clickety-clack

catch a whiff of fermenting grapes
rising from the alleyway cracks
washed down by hose
under asphalt clouds by harvesters
and winemaking neighbors Barristers
at the end with redbrick walls

Midway up the stairs "Door behind me
Close…" it does   Bright gray out window
Final car rolls by Track 63 (year born)
I then go right Key out Go right
Then right and right
into my office

SMALL MATTER

It is a small matter
that I am a writer.
Where is my heart?
Was I born before words?
In a word? Maybe I
was born before words.
Then my heart
would have been
stone? Air?

It is a small matter
that I speak poetry.
The most powerful
poetry is
motion, action.
Why just "think"
and "feel" what you
say?

The mountain
has outlasted words.
The elements
created
all that is,
including us.

I suppose we have aspired
to speak to say
what's on our minds,
to mull over thoughts
and those that aren't our own.

It is a small matter
if we don't see
eye-to-eye.
Now THAT small matter has
created a bigger matter
for us all.

BILLY O'WYLIE: St. Patrick's Day, Celebrating Your Life

for Bill Wylie

The banjo is you and you are the banjo.
Face It, Bill, its face, the strings,
Teeth and guts,
Tender, tenacious, you, its strings,
When played right, plucked, stroked
With acceptable pressure,
Warble like a whitecapped wavefrom river chokeroll,
Sweetpoptartflowing,
Skimming off the strum,
No lies, but capable of long deceptions.

The vibrations of Life transport us
Through piles of rocks or eruptions,
Rolling, falling, tripping,
Moving, displacing rocks
To never put where left,
Rocks on floors of bathrooms,
Gardens, basements, hard
Against glass windows, smash!
Rockstrings rockhard
Thumbs and fingers scramble over
Finn Cool mystical forming song of place
In place still without a place.

When you went arthritic, you still rolled,
No feeling in fingers, you let
Emotions take over and flow from the heart,
Glacial, speaking to another time full of
Rapture, torment, humility, grace,
All under pressure when plucked
From this earth on busride home
Of wrath, heaven's reign, from there,

Nearing here, you, Morning Moon,
Let your eyes close sitting in your Eternal Seat.
No long goodbyes, no lingering note, no
Missed beats, you were always rambling,
Hard to move along through ivory keys.
We settle on speaking your free-wheeling name,
Smirking in the shadows, heart-stopping strings
Heard folding a chord..

SPOKANE SYMPHONY: OPENING NIGHT

with Norvel and Jamie Bear, September 2009

Norvel and I get ready for symphony as
Suzannah my landlord above is serenaded
Home by her friend's violin The notes cry
Through the bedroom furnace vents
Sad yearning for home is what some want
Beyond the pain

At symphony I need coffee A woman cuts in front of me
Norvel shrugs "With this crowd
In particular you have to be quick" I didn't
See it coming He always does
We take our seats I am next to a large strapping man
With his right arm in a sling The woman across
From us is wearing an Edward Gorey skirt
Her legs an entangled collage of black and white
Tree branches specks of stars swirling orbs
The vent wafts cool air in waves
Down across the balcony behind us
Thin lines of perfumes and cologne catch
The air and trickle down

We're all poised for the raptured confusion
Of Bolero—Bolero insistent
Irregular ostinato repeating Sudden unexpected
Change of key More instruments
Meticulous Explosive Masterpiece
As secret as today's headlines
Inspired by dance Boldly confused

"The Star Spangled Banner" takes off
All rise to our patriotic feet I turn to Norvel
And ask "What is this?" as the man next to me

Croons the words of the National Anthem
Bravado Up and Down What so proudly he hails
His wife filling in the higher gaps
After I turn to him and say "You sing beautifully"
He scrunches up his face Speechless
Why would someone comment on singing
The National Anthem   Don't We All Sing It?
He leans in and says "I get to do that once a year
On opening night!"
Show Pride War Cry
Persevere a notion so fraught with
Corruption and Greed We are
Passionate to proclaim
Our own wrongs united in patriot song

"There must be someone new sitting
In the violin second chair" Sling says to his wife
Norvel spots Mia Chang
And even Lily Tomlin I recognize the Cowles
From when I served tables at Fugazzi
In grad school   Sometimes you sense Class

At break the unpretentious French guest pianist
Signs my CD says "Zan is an unusual name"
I ask him if his fingers ever get tired
He says "No they're used to it" I tell him I am
A poet "Music and poetry…" he says slowly

Yes I am inspired as Norvel and I go back
To our seats watch the woodwind section
Raise their flutes from their laps
Place the mouthpieces to their lips
As clarinet and oboe suck on their reeds
Paused prepping with spit to create
Bubbly cracks screams and stabs contained

In the violent course of oceanic curves and curls
Scheherazade   Arabian Nights
The pillaging mindset of Khalif
How dare he rape before killing each wife
Treat women this way It is hard to contain
The barbarous rhythms notes as we ponder what?
Not the beauty of it all

The conductor works up a sweat in four movements
While others are engrossed in rattling the cage
Of their chairs with their programs while others
Turn pages don't talk or look up but squint
Is this why we're in the mess we're in?

Cultures and languages crumble
As people are beheaded and maimed
Blundered and toppled
Exterminated
There are those who sit civil and listen
Take notes even but here the notes take us
Soaring to the ceiling climbing the sky
Sweet fleeting tones string suspended
The mallets of the drum held in pause
Waiting for birth from the belly of the cymbal
Summoning us to take off while
Leaders rule
Without conscience
Broken talks
Council ignored
Demonstrative jihad
Symphony taking us to the brink of
The ends of our worlds

SADIE GOES TO SYMPHONY

Sadie hasn't been out in years.
We can't tell how long
She is breaking a secret
Letting herself out—demanding
To go, so we take her.
Jim T's wife, Carol,
Says, "Really nice bear…"
As I raise Sadie from my bag.
Most stare, after I
Turn to reveal—
They wonder, what?
Who are you dressed in that,
Carrying that?
"Oh, it's Norvel," someone says,
And Sadie waits to be introduced.
It's easy in this crowd
To get overlooked, and
To overlook introducing one
To another.
If you remember names or not,
"Hi" "How are you?" "Why not?"
Beethoven reminds Sadie
Of the cavalry, and things
She says her mother told her
About hiding in a cave
From cavalry men down below,
On a shelf, always on a shelf
Caught up in calling batallions.
War, Sadie says, it's war that
It reminds her of—She wonders
If Wallace is having fun at home
While her ears fill with Barrecco

I find out all season I will sit
Next to Jerry who used to work
Public TV in Yakima.
He's a sweet image of patron
"Bravos" compound the orchestra
Norvel says ask him questions
I say I don't want to intrude
Suddenly I am in touch with
A polite side that wasn't once there
But has been birthed of this evening.
If I let her, Sadie'd set the pace
For some Southern Hospitality
God is South
There is a fugue in the strings
Adding orchestra to statement
Yes, there is a teddy bear
In my bag. Her name is Sadie.
She ate half my candy bar.

DANSE MACABRE: January 7, 2013
Nothing as it seems

for Norvel, RIP

I sleep in 3-hour intervals
wrapped up in every minute
I can get letting
each second encase me
not slip
each time
that alarm goes off
I get up and turn
get up and turn Norvel
and down
the dark

It's up and turn
rub relax
the small of his back
he can't feel
back relax relax back relax
then back on the hide-a-way
not hid away: In
this cocoon room
nothing is as it seems The still
in the twinkling of
Christmas lights is where
transformation looms

I count each breath of his
that gets lost above
and hovering Time is
such a slippery slope
that I
pull a wool cap
over my ears hold Beats

tight to my head plug into
duduk Grief not yet that deep
not yet deep grief

His shallow breath swirls
to the ceiling
to get even with Life
In cocoon room I become
stealthy Comanche planning next moves
keeping closer and closer watch
to next-move-some-move
while all around him is so familiar
yet closer to the
Grand
Flyaway
Hoodoo

ROBERT CAPA MORNING

Winter turns into snow, melts a groggy lens of black & white
into drip drops off slate roofs
into gravel-filled Pacific Street potholes
into gray puddles of grease swirls endless rainbows
into expanding change: rainbows of tinman mind
Nothing interrupts this intimate erosion
no crow is staring into nature's reflection
Close enough, the gurgle of water
streams down gutter spouts
into fast trickles a slip wrist from black to blast
into cigarette after cigarette smoking out the past
bloomboom
bloomboom
bloomboom
click

NOTHING IS EVER FOR SURE...
and everything is always changing

There is an ocean
at the end of
my eyes
that bubbles up
and jumps
white waves
squeezes
the top
of my breath

My burdens
build up and then
crash
flat as salt because
tongue first
is all of you

If I stand
long
my ankles get
sucked into a
slow sink
crashing
and burnt

We all become
dry bones
as Mother Sun
grinds down
beaches
of sand

UNSETTLED

for Jamie Wyeth

Is the abyss
the light side of darkness?
What haunts us
is a white owl in the snow
We can see
it is what
disturbs our passions
butchers our hearts
in waves of blood
our veins a brine
of Red Sea
until we are pillars
of salt-faceted
crystals screen
see-throughs

Unsettled
is seeing through ourselves
until there's nothing left
to do but spiral outward
Unsettled
is a stroke
of generational genius
deep as dirt
kaledoscopic
awake and asleep
It is a blank canvas or page
awaiting brush of word
It's buried out back
with the bones
I don't and I do

I am ready I am not
Unsettled
is love at its tightest about to split
at the seams and bursting out
confined clandestine

Unsettled
is the twist of a sail
in crisp salt air the cock
of a gull's wing cutting
through the grayest of sky
as a curve of new direction
spirals
Upward and over
Upward and wave
Upon wave
Upon wave
of goodbyes

V

EIGHT, AND IT: TAG ON 72ND AVE

for the Ippoliti Family

Standing frozen
in the middle of the street
in front of my house
the world goes spinning
around me
the rest of my friends scatter
even Eddie Adams
can't be seen
Where do I begin to search
for bodies limbs sticking out
from familiar unfamiliar
places: bushes garages we
shouldn't be in
Mrs. Schmidt's backyard
is a refuge How far
have they gone to elude me
make it impossible
to be found? In this
game the goal is to
act like you're missing
make as though you're gone for good
There is tension frustration fear
that rises from the bottom up
I'll get you Claire!
The competition manifests itself
in the ultimate conquest
of creeping up on one of them
reaching quick into thin air
to touch one of them
yelling
Tag you're IT!
Going through the list of who all is out there

Tripping upon one of them making too much
noise rustling hiding
somewhere nervous
Behind a new neighbor's back door
Trespassing: a major motivator
to outtrick me as I stumble and whirl
the sun going down the sidewalks we
play jacks on ride our bikes down jump rope chalk up
I fall to my knees in excitement out of breath
Quick stand up brush hopscotch off my hands
That was Barbara Ann down their driveway
through the honeysuckle bushes clinging to the cyclone fence
Whispers and laughter translate to
A-ha whoever you are you are caught!
It's Little Teresa the youngest so cute
grabbing out from the blossoms sprigs and stems
just as Aunt Mary her mother opens
the kitchen door wide quickly asking
What are you kids up to now?
I'm the perpetrator full of shame
yet triumphant put my hand out
sweep it down my cousin's back laughing
Tag you're IT!
Now where's that Claire BarbBran chubby Eddie
and his sinister sister Denise?

WATCH MY MONEY: A Phone Call with Bill Deery

for my father

My father tells me
Watch my money,
How I spend it,
Everything costs.
You can have it
One minute
And NOT
The next

Like dying
And life,
I think, or
Having love, and
In a flash, gone.

Have you done
Your taxes?
Yes, I owe.
Eleven hundred
Dollars.

You owe? How could you?
You are unemployed.

I took all of my pay upfront,
Dad, took it all.
And now, I owe.

You should have let them
Take a little at a time,
Then you wouldn't
Owe so much.

Well, I didn't do it that way
Because I needed it all.
If I let them take it,
I would have had less,
In fact,
Not enough
To live on...Anyway,
What are you having for dinner?

Oh, he sighs, *You know your mother...*
Dorothy? He yells into what I assume
Is the kitchen, her in it:
What are we having tonight,
Darlin' Dorothy? His voice
All roses and quivers.

I roll my eyes at the embedded memory
Of what this all looks like:
I am right there
Catching their dance

At the end of a wedding,
Many times, the last two
On the floor, cutting the rug,
Making it happen/making a point/
We have survived!

They are the Ones
Whose purpose is to reveal
To others that this is it,
This is how to live!

I feel my age, Sandra,
Sandy, I feel my age.

This time of night,
Lying here, I feel my age.
I'm ready for the retirement home—
The Vet Retirement Home.
I've already put in a reservation.
I'm on their list.

This is why we never know
What my dad is thinking.

Really. I'm not kidding you.
Where Byberry used to be.
They're putting in
A vet's home.

Are you eligible for that?

Elig—of course, I'm a vet, Sandra.

So, you can get a place…a room
With a great view…A view…

Of the Boulevard
Overlooking NABISCO,
The neon N

Well, I want to go to the driving range
With you when I come.

We'll see, Sandy. We'll see.

No, really, I want to do that with you.

Sandy, you know it could get—
As Dad hands the phone to Mom

She wants to go to the driving range.
I've said all I need to say
And I hope you get something
Out of it, Sandy. Look, I'm gonna go now.
So nice to talk with you.
Yes, Sandra, Love you, too.
Good night!
Oh, your mother says,
Give ItZy a kiss, from her.

Okay…All right…Good Night

MY ANGEL

for Dorothy Deery

My mother makes angels of herself,
desires, wishes, who wouldn't
at Eighty-Seven? Who wouldn't regret they
hadn't done it at least once
in their lives?
Talk to angels, why not?
She prays for me and my dog,
to Norvel, to
watch over us. She

says he's my guardian angel
and I envision Norvel in the nude
dangling from above in Bauhaus-retro
ultra-thin wing blades,
a Perpetual Light Meter. She

asks him for favors. Isn't that
what you do with angels?
He can cover
so much territory we can't.
He's so hyper-ultra,
I won't dismiss her desperate grace,
forsaking my own.

See,
I don't even pray to Norvel that much.
Hell, I'll pray to things
and people I know nothing about. Does
it make those prayers any lesser?

I still say his name. I'm sure he'd
understand dismissal
if I had to count.

What reminds me of him, or others?
Who are the goneforgoods, signs of the crosses?
There better be
plenty of angelic power to go around

because

we all could use a walk around the world
each day halfway, a foot in this world,
a foot in that, a step back in history
of ancestors, mentors,
elders, lovers, friends.

And so

if my mother walks with angels
in her prayers and pictures,
and one of
them is NorvelLeeNorvel,
then here I fly low in a realm,
                    welcoming this murmuring embrace,
                    this daily
                              churn to ashes
                              to gain wings.

THE AMNESTY BOX*: War Song for David

Take this song and do what is custom: toss it in that box *my war is gone* We all want the same at first but then the flight of greed crashes into our lives No knocks or warnings just barges in riding a bigoted cold spiral wave We all have medicine to kill ourselves well enuf with thanks Isn't that what War's friends think? What the fuck money spent Think nothing of not responding Why blame them? If they don't someone else will get there first So where you rank now? You used to sit on the Cabinet Now you're hiding Pol Pot? When did he come out? How hungry is his ghost today? Bones? I hear the Dalai Lama wants to quit his job World's full of fake news Dude What a name for a prick huh? I'll look him up draw a moustache on his face with evil horns out his head(s) call him expletives: pension annuity benefits taxed add insult to injury paint that box blue the porn drugs and contraband inside now theirs: smooth oblivion gone Always free for them to gamble their Horserace of War with Trifecta the headache out

**Amnesty Boxes are sealed containers that enable visitors to anonymously dispose of contraband/non-permissible items, without fear of detection or arrest, before entering restricted areas.*

SUNDAY MORNING HAIRCUTS WITH DAVID: UNDER THE KENSINGTON EL, PHILLY

My brother is a smiling Buddha
In the barber chair at Vin's

He is in Vietnamese Heaven
All around him, Vin swings and sways his bamboo broom
In swift, tight, circles around the bases of the chairs
Pushing shaved hair from the floor
Into an oversized dustpan

True love's as old as war

Nothing is stained as us and almost everything
Else outside under the clutter of the El is
Kensington needled Avenue
Getting flooded by sudden storm beyond form
The front window of the shop fogs up

Vin pops the door and the smell of rust and gas
Drops down and stirs up in a wave of warm air:
An Impressionistic painting

David is tipped back face wide as the Cheshire Cat
Lin takes her hands and starts rubbing his cheeks in circles
It reminds me that it's an illusion we need hair on our heads,
That we all live separate lives That beards can come off

Afterwards and outside, I turn to my brother and warn
To watch out for all the needles on the ground,
Especially wearing only sandals,
Whodoyouthinkyouare, Jesus?

MOM'S LAMENT

The silence between here and there,
I call it, where she stares at a label
She's seen a thousand times and
Wonders what it says, where it came from

Who am I now, and why is this here?
What is this messed-up existence
That used to be my life where I
Called my own shots
Faked my own death Fell asleep in front of the TV
For as long as I wanted
Walked where I wanted to walk,
Ate what the hell I pleased—got it myself

How the hell, who the hell
How in God's, who in God's name,
Why did he do this to me?
Why doesn't he listen to me?
Is he there? Maybe not.
Nobody cares! Bill?
Bill, take me!

ZAN'S LAMENT
(Best Sung Outside a Childhood Window)

Open up that window, child
Let the rain come cryin' in
Dripping' off the cedar, Mama,
Let it in, come cryin' in
Trees my Mama loved
(Inside her) Let the rain
Come cryin in Soon I'm
Gonna tell my brother,
He'll say, "Hell, just let it in!"
Leaves gone fallin' in
The gutters, down the roof,
And on the lawn
Rattlin' bones I hear them tremble
'round like Mama's
Bones gone Wind
Bones and ashes gone blown
'round November sun
Stretched on the ground
Casting shadows 'til the
Evening 'til the morning
Dawn comes on—Branches
Stretch like arms around
Arms around
House arrest is real as hell.

THE LOVESEAT COUCH in My Parents' House

When I stare at it now from across their living room,
Morning sun spots it brightly and if I look close enough
A thin pattern of branches cast shadows onto the olive
Back curve of the couch

Three lacey pillows stretch across it, implying that
Three people can fit on it

I remember Christmases when visitors would attempt
To find comfort on that couch but with its shallow seat
Hardly did one fit unless one sat up straight
Even my brother would attempt to curl up on it
But never found comfort from it Hardly anyone in my family found
Much comfort or love on it except for my parents
They'd sit there opening Christmas presents showing us,
"This is how it's done..."

My parents (now I) have many photos to prove it
Tuck yourselves away on it in the corner,
Accept photos on it, conversation with others
From the floor looking up, you get a
Good view behind from the rug of the wooden plaquard
Bust silhouettes of George and Martha Washington

Why? No wonder so much here seems so anchored
So full of history and mystery   Stable force
Who will it sell to? How will it end up?
The future of Love, from this angle, is grim,
The way everything goes wrong in Hamilton
David and I only feel we are doing what is Right
For the family Say, whatever, really, is left to own,

Outright,
But the love we had? And even then,
Gone if we don't remember and claim?

A HOLD ON MORNING: THE MIDDLE ROOM

The twinkling white lights of
Christmas lie before me galaxies
Of memories countless drops of
Light like rain on a windshield
A dark room childhood unbound
And not all far away
Praying over many rivers
For a right heart
We cry unrestrained as bass strings:
We think we know but tough
We don't know No matter how hard
It gets We try Life lives on a page
Words die in old dog warm in blanket
Waiting for the tidal recipe for happiness
To present itself

The morning sun glows through
The windows of the middle room
Branches tap slap the lower roof
Over the garage, a love song
From the Backyard Symphony
Trees my mother loves
Maybe it's a call we haven't made for years
Pause
Maybe it leaves us in suspended animation
With twisted hopeless resolves
Too deep to ride the Tilt-a-Whirl
Or let that kind of ride get you down
Oh, man, coffee drive-thru
Year after Year Sometimes dark
Sometimes extra cream ocean bubbles
From an incoming wave swallowed me up

Punched up sorrow sunken treasure
The bittersweet moan of tomorrow coming
Beautifully holding Mom, alone

ONE OF THE FORGOTTEN

My mantra is *go gentle*
into that dark night each day
I pay *such* attention
Can you, me or anyone ever be forgiven?
I am our (my) father,
and that's why my mother votes for me.
At 86, she wants Change.
I'm no patriot,
can't box me like that.
I doubt I'll ever understand the World.
Most people don't even *like* poetry.

Sure, I watched that show with "him,"
believe me, I was unemployed and broke
in the Recession, I'd lip synch, *You're fired!*
just so I could feel important,
feel something other than myself crumbling.

The Show is much bigger now,
more at stake, the wildfires
larger, and smoke more frequent.
Suddenly, they get to fire
whomever the fuck they want.

Is there a criterion for being forgotten?
'Cause I ain't no joiner.
One thing's for certain,
I didn't come out of my mother's womb
to be guarded by a military police.
I've learned a thing or two being born
in the Land of Deception
and Zippity Do-Da
all Day.

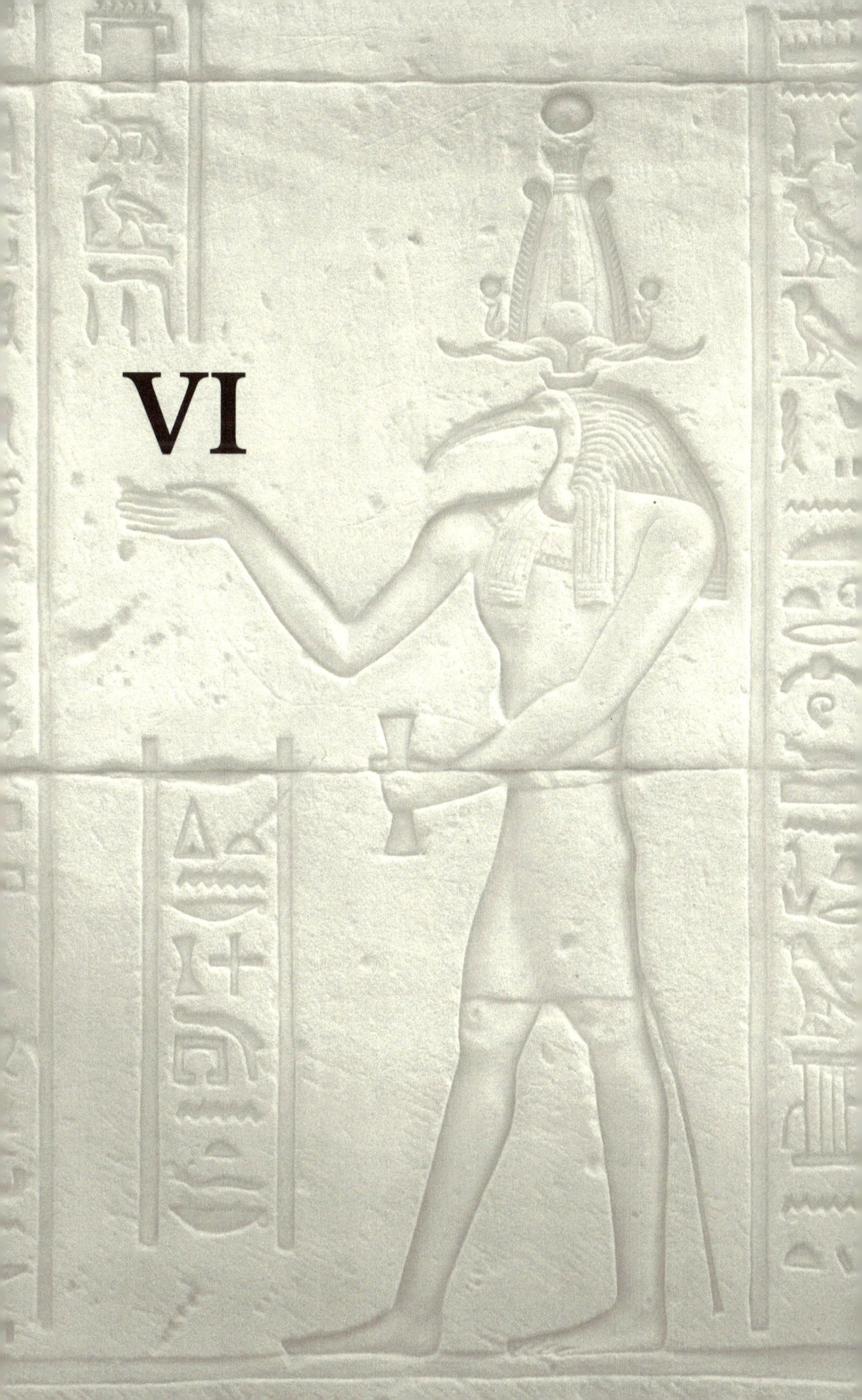

VI

ZENA

for Louise "Zena" Gryting

You, I've
reversed my journey so
the bad does not see worse.
Reverse to be born unrehearsed,
an opposite road leading
who knows where we go

missing hard into rock,
back to black basalt, again
beginning, morphed in a breath,
life's swift hello-goodbye.

No longer are you ice cream
on a bench on a pier
under a full Green Lake moon.

Seattle is no longer "Zen"
bent over pregnant blackberries.
                    We are
not brambles down a dark I-5
tingling in fog dense mud,
lost dreams of huddling
Makah rising up swollen ocean
swells in canoes of cedar,
whale in sight, tail up and out.

**

You're clinging to this world
cold coat on metal chair,
closet empty, linoleum gleaming…

I am drenched in dismal.
I kiss any dusty relic
held before my lips.
My own cross hangs
within limits, face
posing lessons by demons.
I fly demons, my painkiller. I'll die
Myowndie for Baby Blue.

**

Minute agents of dragged-out
mortality told me "The Pope is dead," the TV's broken prayer.
"How much" she asked, "does he have to die?"
"The Pope is dead" over and over
"The Pope is dead."

Harp a person to death,
our cultural epiphany
drives our prolific
hospice beds into dirt.
I want to lull you, Zena, gasping
these earthly words into life.

I have eternity to read
the letters you handed me
in that box, unsent.

How does spirit wave
gray memory
quiet as a drowned tomb?

A gurgling creek of oxygen
trickles in the middle
of night while I
kick back on ethereal

couch in light celestial
watching your shoulder
lean on flat pillow, Time.

**

Neighborhood rooster
crows, his talons click
on metal roof, his doodle-
do pierces this foxhole
collapsing around me, and parts us,
friends to the end. I lay back along
your legs, soft space gobbles like
a clock.

A dream, where I was,
of late lessons learned now. That
once upon waking, dream watching,
you pay piper a tune or two,
a drowning not tied to rock,
sacrificed for a Queen,
pawn of this dawn. I'm
rowing an ocean,
deep day sailing,
this window-surrounded couch
drips restraint. Lake Washington is crying.

**

Tickety-tick, tick-tock
Tickety tick, tick tock,
blown and kicked about by wind,
turbulent, your labored breath
not afraid to lock words to salt.

I try to give you something.
You need nothing. You give me something.
I need everything.

**

Across the street, at the French bakery—
I choose everything: glazed tart,
brioche, buttersweet
birth of another morning
in our awake.

Had to tell them to stop
filling the brown box
landing overfull bittersweet brim
with my dues. I climb the stairs
to the belly of the whale.

**

In the parking lot, in my rental car, Jimmy Cliff
gives me love, the weight of it all
with this birthday CD you gave me.
I play it everywhere I go,

Many rivers to crossss—oo—osss—
and it's only my will that keeps me a liiiii-iiii—ive…

I wish you free-flow on a river
from the mountains to the ocean
connecting your channel
to places without pain, weightless
headwater without me. You struggled
to live, to stay alive,
to swallow in a whirlpool,
our life force down drainage.

**

I sit stark in the middle,
testament to unconditional

wrath of rocky reach, stroke by stroke,
of tunneled white parking lot light,
box of pastries in my lap.

I smoke in this empty spot,
white puffs curl tight off my breath,
chilled
against raindrops that pattern
the windshield. I rehearse slow,
half-goodbyes to the color of my
colossal horse
off the black square of this game,
past the towering castle
traversed across our
special niche.

I
place the brown carton between your knees.
You pass on each sweet shape.
I am already sick from eating too many.
On my short life,
I grasp and gorge.

**

In random, yet prolific rites
of passage to obscure channels
of identity, imaginary doors slam.
I rant my wrongs like a drunk
to the silent dark, the only capable
opening. Double beam me up,
standing in this shallow
creek saturated up to my knees
in cold with love.

In the gift shop
porcelain angels lined up
on a shelf, no eyes, what gives?

Aspire to be a Gandhi,
rich with a view of Virginia City
up a desolate street
shaped "H" for Hope? We have been
to other moons, always
wanted one to fit in my pocket.
Now you have many round spoons
feeding your days pounded out like dents.
Make me your pain's Oxycotin.

**

I promise to be no addict,
but memorable. I stare
outside the window, want to be
the squirrel leaping that high wire,
turning each angle of a pinecone
searching for pinyons with answer seeds.
Let's meet up a branch
like that, over potent answers,
one night on a long tightrope,
quivering recess of river below
the collision of force. Scamper up to
unknown windows, peer in
with skewed sight.
I never had to put so many
last words to what we were,
never needed to explain shame.

**

The everlasting oceanic cosmos
is locked in Kabbalah clamshells

the way today's slacking tide
slides open, and closes,
glistening and gliding,
enveloping grains
of sand rolling in foam balls
of steel gray mercury
across jade storm dreams.

I am shelled out bottom,
not near the underneath
of it all, because today is my last
day in this clandestine net
floating on grace. Our lips will not
speak where we speak only yarrow,
Russian thistle, marjoram, camas root,
where garlic cluster messages fight
with organized bondage of
clover-spiced lapses
that will burst a final heat as
your vein refuses the needle.

**

Today is a tumbling cervix,
undulating vortex
of our universe
birthing frequencies,
certain that transgressions
of flesh ache deep
until there's no breath. Zena,
that childhood story
when bighorn rams perched high
above mine-crested rock shelves,
hometown planks overhanging
Morenci, Arizona. It was early morning
when you caught them in the copper dusted

dawn, stealthily balancing, countenance nimble
on unpredictable slate,
firm hooves covered in Apache dirt.

**

Like following a recipe,
Dotson and I scattered your ashes,
each key ingredient, step by step,
into a box, parts
we let fly like swallows,
swooping, dipping Southwest wind.

**

In the high-rolling Sitgreaves
dripping abandon
we tossed the dust of you out and over
that empty trail, horse cliff,
Dear Girl, it was
Easter, dawn.

**

Dotson took pictures of me
releasing you for daughter, Sheri,
on the high plains desert, cold
daybreak hovering over dayrock
piles, slipping in sandy soil,
panicky thimbles of resurrection,
air arresting time as ants
at my feet built stronger pile fort
hills higher than me, deeper
than tunnel of self-worth. Sense
and order came in the chandelier
effect of bone fragments
hitting spring facet, crumbs scant
ocean/desert born in reverse.

**

You warm me to have known you.
I loved to go through
your picture albums with you. Now, today,
it only makes me miss you.

Can it be true: 'til death do we part?
So when one parts, the other parts, too?
No matter how much we reverse,
we live in rehearse.

To where you go may we
all go home
earth-glossed placentas
no longer bleeding.
May this too pass
us by hell. We don't need
to argue with the cosmos
speeding by
too fast.

**

Outside your one-room
Phelps Dodge miner's cabin,
Mother's pushing
you on a safe swing from harm
up to heaven.

BLESSED MOTHER AND OUR FATHER:
Last Morning, on the Back Porch

for my siblings and brother-in-law, Pete

I
Allpowerful allmighty
You both rise from my throat
Like a pomegranate opening up
Revealing its juices and seeds
Veins of life packed neat
Bursting through
A sky blue lets new air in
Quan Yin incense glows
Old and final in a piece of pottery
On the window sill
Evoking the glow of birthday
Candles, fireflies flashing
Beyond the back porch screens
Fresh-cut deli meats on a tray
On the picnic table out here
Shower Queen
Now tranquility dates
This back room
Showers it with
Compassion and Truth
An indigo wave of Life
Flashes across the ceiling
Dodging the hanging lamps
And cabin seashell mobiles
Bamboo loops masking
The true chains they hang from
A few spiderwebs
Duck under the ripples
On the wood panels
Flush to the brick
You always said Don't kill them

II
Barefoot cold and full of night
I showed up because you told me
We might go under the dark
And even get ripped away
Trying to find Life
In the things we can't:
It's a fat contract

It might be like Daumal
At a Séance searching for
That intense world of eternity
And for real we'll feel the burn

I can only imagine
A concentrated flame
And in runs ItZy as though
Feeling the Burn looking
Like she has entered into
Another layer of knowledge

III
I am feeling Heaven in my hands
Placing my palm on the head
Of a statue of Jesus my mother
Has here on the porch
Every morning I lifted Jesus
By the head and made a doorstop
Out of him Made him useful
Put him to work for All of Us
He helped let air in from the outside
To cool the house

I'm feeling my mom and my dad
In the trees through the ground

Through the warped kitchen floor
The falling-apart brick BBQ
On the side of the house
I can't put a chair outside
Without thinking summer parties
And paper flower decorations
Drooping with glee
From the branches out back
Betsy Ross is in these trees
As I watch two mighty geese
Rocket across the cosmic
Landscape of recall
Some unresolved purgatories
Ripple freely waiting to be
Chased and spanked
The brats that they are It's all lined
Up for release from the anguished twist
This place of Being
A phantasmagoria
Leading to discovery
Grand and clear
When was the last time I had
An epiphany? Maybe never
This one POW

IV
The end of the world was my mother
Gunshy with my dad gone
The nights creeping up on her
What more she couldn't do
Resilient even if her grocery list
Was desperately redundant
With Splenda
When in the pantry were boxes
Of 100/40/200

And there was my Father
Who Art in Heaven
Camp Hart be thy Name
Two Tricksters in Death
As David and ItZy and I
Make our way
Out the Door
For good

V
A crow lands two more
On the branch of a locust:
Trifecta Bill
Reminding us to not believe
All of what you hear and don't
Think you know because
Most of the times you don't

The house is full of songs
Transcending time
They move through the bedrooms
Living room den
Come on the radio
As Philly HYY Classical
Crown Deli hoagies
Become
Manna for the Road
Early on a Sunday morn
Even the all-women's
Deli counter crew
Get crying when
I tell them our story
They tuck cookies
And sliced liverwurst
For ItZ

Say
"You and your brother come back to see us
Sometime"

Walking out looking
Over the stretch of
Morrell Plaza Shopping
Center parking lot
There's Mom's bank
Charlie's Pizza David says
They've gone downhill
Since moving here
From Roosevelt Boulevard
It's official now Old
Neighborhood No More
This bag weighs a ton
Anybody got some
Kumbaya?
Wha Baya
Wha Kum
Amen?

Also by Zan Agzigian:

Stamen and Whirlwind

ABOUT THE AUTHOR

photo: Norvel Trosst

Zan is a poet, story writer, playwright and arts advocate. She worked in collaboration with Bitterroot Salish MT poet Victor Charlo, co-writing Native plays, which have been performed throughout the Northwest. Zan received grants to cultivate, nurture and promote Native Theater in Indian Country. *Stamen and Whirlwind*, her first book of poetry, was published in 2008 by Gribble Press. She holds an MFA in Fiction from EWU and lives in Vinegar Flats, Spokane,WA. Zan produces and hosts a weekly music mix show, *Soundspace*, for Spokane Public Radio, and works for the Better Business Bureau Great West + Pacific.

ENDNOTE

Drawing down the reservoir to pay homage to those times and the people,
a vast landscape, a fast 15-year fantasia breaking grief through stone.

These poems praise what now softly strokes my dreams and memory,
and now will yours, I hope. Like a big band, timeless, nostalgic—
a legacy jitterbug, rainbows, black and whites, lost and not lost souls
remain as transcendent souls land and sing their songs: eerie and divine.

This collection was drummed up soaking wet with toil and tears,
years of grappling rhyme to retrieve the years that are gone.

There is a sweet desperation to rekindle the Heart of it All,
the Be to Be, those moments of becoming a channel for
the Eternity of Truth I know and don't know.

The longer I live and write, the more I question the miracle
of the Last Breath—It's a poem all its own that can't be
given a word but can be felt.

It's a beginning at the End that is so poignant, it
takes no reservations, but tells what is Right because
it's really all grounded in Love. Then, let go.

Z.A. April 1, 2026,
Spokane, WA

www.ingramcontent.com/pod-product-compliance
Lightning Source LLC
LaVergne TN
LVHW051002080826
845145LV00009B/2404

* 9 7 8 1 9 6 2 9 3 4 0 4 6 *